CUPS, BOWLS, AND OTHER
FOOTBALL CHAMPIONSHIPS

RICHARD BLAINE

CRABTREE
Publishing Company
www.crabtreebooks.com

D1214474

FOOTBALL SOURCE

Author: Richard Blaine

Editors: Marcia Abramson, Petrice Custance

Photo research: Melissa McClellan

Design: T.J. Choleva

Cover design: Samara Parent

Proofreader: Janine Deschenes

Editorial director: Kathy Middleton

Prepress technician: Samara Parent

Print coordinator: Margaret Amy Salter

Consultant: R Ian Smith. President.
Ontario Football Alliance

Production coordinated by BlueAppleWorks Inc.

Cover image: Georgia Tech Yellow Jacket players celebrate after winning the Capital One Orange Bowl Game in 2014.
Title page image: The running back from the University of Maryland's Terrapins tries to squeeze through a hole in the Temple Owls.

Photographs
Cover: Associated Press: ©Icon Sportswire via AP Images
Interior: Corbis: © PCN/Corbis (p 20); Shutterstock.com: © dean bertoncelj (title page); Richard Paul Kane (title page middle); © wavebreakmedia (TOC); pbombaert (page numbers); © Steve Broer (TOC background); © Richard Paul Kane (p 8–9 top); © Noel Moore (p 8–9 bottom, 12–13 bottom); © Mat Hayward (p 12–13 top); © Action Sports Photography (p 16); © Alexey Stiop (p 20–21 bottom); © Nando Machado (p 27 bottom); Herbert Kratky (p 28 top left, 28 bottom left); © tammykayphoto (p 30); Keystone Press: © Louis Lopez (p 7); © Michael Prengler (p 9 top); © Charles Baus (p 10 left); © Bob Larson (p 19 right); Library of Congress Prints and Photographs: Warren K. Leffler (p 13 top); Public Domain: p 4; John Singer Sargent (p 5 left); p 5 top right; p 5 bottom right; Official White House Photo by Pete Souza (p 8); U.S. Navy photo by Damon J. Moritz (p 11 right); p 12 bottom left; Malcolm W.Emmons (p 13 bottom); Lance Cpl. Ethan Hoaldridge (p 21 top right); p 25 top; Creative Commons: MECU (p 9 left); Jakesthesnake (p 10 right); Neon Tommy (p 11 left); The rakish fellow (p 12 top left); soldiersmediacenter (p 14); Alan Kotok (p 15); andrewtat94 (p 17); John Tornow (p 19 left top); US Embassy Canada (p 19 left bottom); Mahanga (p 20–21 top); Mike Morbeck (p 21 left); Jeffrey Beall (p 21 bottom right); mark.watmough (p 22); Cmm3 (p 23); Dan Dickinson (p 24); Roland Tanglao (p 25 bottom); AleXXw (p 26, 28–29 top, 28–29 bottom, 29 top left, 29 bottom left); Pierre-Yves Beaudouin (p 27 top); wobblecam (p 29 top right); Photofest: p 18 left; 18 right

Library and Archives Canada Cataloguing in Publication

Blaine, Richard, author
    Cups, bowls, and other football championships / Richard Blaine.

(Football source)
Includes index.
Issued in print and electronic formats.
ISBN 978-0-7787-2293-9 (bound).--ISBN 978-0-7787-2300-4 (paperback).--ISBN 978-1-4271-1729-8 (html)

    1. Football--Tournaments--Juvenile literature. 2. Super Bowl--Juvenile literature. I. Title.

GV954.B53 2016   j796.332'64   C2015-907468-1
                                          C2015-907469-X

Library of Congress Cataloging-in-Publication Data

CIP available at the Library of Congress

Crabtree Publishing Company
www.crabtreebooks.com   1-800-387-7650

Printed in Canada/012016/BF20151123

Published in Canada
Crabtree Publishing
616 Welland Ave.
St. Catharines, ON
L2M 5V6

Published in the United States
Crabtree Publishing
PMB 59051
350 Fifth Avenue, 59th Floor
New York, New York 10118

Published in the United Kingdom
Crabtree Publishing
Maritime House
Basin Road North, Hove
BN41 1WR

Published in Australia
Crabtree Publishing
3 Charles Street
Coburg North
VIC 3058

CONTENTS

WIN THE DAY!

FOOTBALL TAKES OFF

How football began depends on who you ask. Some believe the sport goes all the way back to the game of Harpastum, which was played by the ancient Greeks and Romans. Points were awarded when a player kicked, passed, or ran a ball past a goal line. Since the players did not have equipment, injuries were common. Football is also closely linked to rugby, which was invented at Rugby School in England in 1830.

Walter Camp, the Father of American Football

If you're looking for one person to thank for football, Walter Camp is your man. Camp invented the line of scrimmage (the spot where the ball is snapped) and the **system of downs**. He also is credited with inventing the offensive backfield, which consists of a quarterback, two halfbacks, and a fullback. Every time a center snaps the ball to a quarterback, they are executing an idea Walter Camp championed.

*Walter Camp studied medicine and worked in the watchmaking business, but his passion was football. He played, coached, and wrote many of the rules. He was **inducted** into the College Hall of Fame as a coach.*

President Teddy Gets Involved

While football's popularity skyrocketed in the late 1800s, so did injuries. In 1905, 18 players were killed in games played in the United States. That same year, President Theodore "Teddy" Roosevelt arranged a meeting of officials from Harvard, Yale, and Princeton. A few months later, 62 schools met in New York City to adopt rules in order to reduce injuries. They formed an association later named the National Collegiate Athletic Association (NCAA).

Players had no helmets and little protective gear in early football.

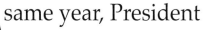

Theodore Roosevelt, 26th president of the United States, had a son who played football at Harvard.

Making the Game Safer

Since protective equipment was still quite new, the only way to make the game safer was to **minimize** the number of collisions. Rules were introduced that cut down on contact. The most important measure, the creation of the **forward pass**, would become a spectacular part of the game. **Roughing the passer** was brought into the rulebook in 1914 as the sport's popularity continued to grow.

Many football players began wearing helmets made of leather in the 1920s.

5

COLLEGE GAME GROWS

College football became very popular in the late 1800s, and the number of teams in the United States grew quickly. For easier scheduling of games, teams were grouped into conferences. Two of the first conferences formed were the Big Ten and the Pacific-12. The Big Ten Conference was formed in 1896 and included teams from the **Midwest**. The Pacific-12 Conference still boasts four of the original members from its first season in 1915: the University of California, the University of Oregon, Oregon State University, and Washington State University.

Divisions

Today, there are over 70 college football conferences. The NCAA groups teams into divisions based on their skill and strength level. There are even subdivisions within the divisions to make sure teams with the same level of talent play each other. The Division I Football Bowl Subdivision (FBS) is the highest level of college football, and has the most scholarships to offer players. There are 11 conferences and over 120 teams in this division.

Bowls Aplenty

Bowl games are postseason games played mostly by Division 1 FBS college teams. The first bowl game took place in 1902 as part of a sports festival called the Tournament of Roses in Pasadena, California. When the Rose Bowl stadium opened in 1923, the Tournament of Roses became known as the Rose Bowl. By 1935, other cities had begun hosting college bowls, and the number kept growing.

Marcus Mariota, quarterback for the Oregon Ducks, shows off his team's 2015 Rose Bowl trophy.

In 2015, the NCAA had 41 bowl games on its schedule! Some of the most famous ones are the Rose Bowl; the Sugar Bowl in New Orleans; the Orange Bowl in Miami Gardens, Florida; the Cotton Bowl in Arlington, Texas; the Fiesta Bowl in Tempe, Arizona; and the Peach Bowl in Atlanta, Georgia.

CATCH THIS!

The Rose Bowl, with room for nearly 93,000 fans, is the biggest as well as the oldest college bowl stadium.

7

WHO'S THE CHAMPION?

For more than 80 years, the nation's top college football teams have been determined through a vote by sportswriters from around the country. The vote began in 1934, due to the fact that in many different conferences and divisions top teams were not able to meet in bowl games. Now, since top teams do meet in a playoff, it is valued more for its in-season rankings.

Bowl Championship Series

In an effort to make sure the best teams were able to play each other, a five-game playoff system was instituted in 2013. Many critics are still unhappy with elements of the setup. Even President Barack Obama, a big college football fan, said he would like to see changes.

Photographers caught President Barack Obama playing a little football with his dog, Bo, on the White House lawn.

College Football Playoff

The goal of the NCAA has always been to have the best two teams in the country play for a national championship. Beginning in 2014, the College Football Playoff (CFP) used a poll of 13 people to choose the top four teams in the nation. The teams then faced off in **semifinal** games, with the final two meeting for the CFP National Championship Trophy. Ohio State won the trophy the first year it was awarded.

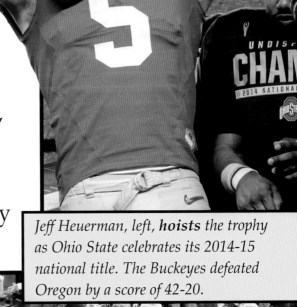

*Jeff Heuerman, left, **hoists** the trophy as Ohio State celebrates its 2014-15 national title. The Buckeyes defeated Oregon by a score of 42-20.*

The Heisman Trophy

The Heisman Trophy has been college football's top individual award since 1935. It is named for John Heisman, a hall of fame coach. The award honors the best player in the NCAA Division 1 Football Bowl Subdivision. Only one player, Ohio State running back Archie Griffin, has won twice (1974 and 1975).

The player on the trophy is not John Heisman. It is modeled after Ed Smith, a leading college player and friend of the sculptor.

COLLEGE FOOTBALL RIVALRIES

Part of the fun of college football are the traditional **rivalries** that go back as far as the 1890s. The winning school takes home bragging rights and often a very unique trophy. Most colleges have at least one big rivalry, and fans will root against their school's rival no matter who they are playing! Some of college football's biggest rivalries involve schools that are closely located to each other. The annual game between the University of Michigan Wolverines and their Midwest neighbors, the Ohio State Buckeyes, is considered one of the fiercest of college football's many rivalries.

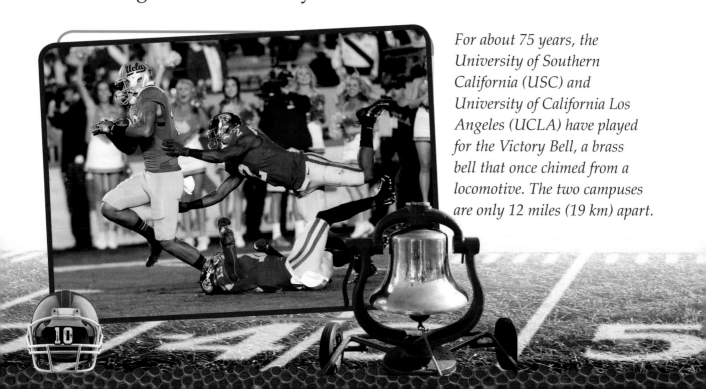

For about 75 years, the University of Southern California (USC) and University of California Los Angeles (UCLA) have played for the Victory Bell, a brass bell that once chimed from a locomotive. The two campuses are only 12 miles (19 km) apart.

Notre Dame-USC Football Rivalry

Despite the huge distance between them, the Fighting Irish of Notre Dame University in Indiana and the Trojans of the University of Southern California have become huge rivals. Both schools have top football programs and fans all over the country, so their games draw a big audience on television. The winner is awarded the Jeweled Shillelagh, a traditional Irish wooden club that bears the name of the winning team from every game.

The Notre Dame-USC football rivalry, which began in 1926, is considered one of the most important in college football. Notre Dame leads the series with 45 wins, 36 losses, and six ties.

The Army-Navy Game

Once a year, teams from the United States Military Academy (USMA) and the United States Naval Academy (USNA) meet in the famous Army-Navy Game. The game is the final scheduled game of the major college football season, and has been played for more than 125 years.

The rivalry between the USMA team, the Army Black Knights, and the USNA team, the Navy Midshipmen, is one of the most fierce and long-lasting rivalries in college football.

11

THE RISE OF THE NFL

The National Football League (NFL) was born at a meeting of football-loving businessmen in a car dealership in Canton, Ohio, in 1920. First called the American Professional Football Conference, the league was renamed the National Football League two years later. Two of the first NFL teams, the Green Bay Packers and Chicago Bears, have built up a rivalry as fierce as any in college football. They first played in 1921, and now meet at least twice a year as divisional rivals in the NFL. Fans always expect the games to be rough, because both teams have proud traditions of winning. Green Bay has won 13 NFL championships while Chicago has nine.

The founder of the Chicago Bears, George Halas (above) was nicknamed "Papa Bear." He won six championships in 40 years of owning and coaching his team.

Growing West

The popularity of the NFL grew steadily after World War II. NFL owners were quick to see the potential in expanding their game into the western United States, leading to the addition of the

Professional football has always attracted large crowds, but during the NFL's early years college football was more popular than the professional version.

Los Angeles Rams in 1946 and the San Francisco 49ers in 1949. By the 1960s, the NFL was a 16-team league thanks to a new team in Dallas. Just like in college football, the NFL decided to divide its teams into conferences. Cleveland, New York, Philadelphia, Pittsburgh, St. Louis, and Washington combined to create the Eastern Conference; while Baltimore, Chicago, Green Bay, Detroit, Los Angeles, San Francisco, and Dallas made up the Western Conference.

Johnny Unitas, known as "The Golden Arm," set many records for passing.

The Greatest Game Ever Played

Many say the greatest game in NFL history was the 1958 championship game in which the Baltimore Colts and their star quarterback, Johnny Unitas, beat the New York Giants 23-17. The Colts' victory was the first ever in overtime, and Unitas's drive for the winning touchdown was a masterpiece of play-calling. Most importantly, the game was watched by a national television audience who were left talking for days about the exciting finish.

13

MIGHTY NFL

Pro football gained many fans in the 1950s, thanks to exciting games like the 1958 championship. For the first time, football could be enjoyed at home as more people began purchasing TV sets. As fans **clamored** for more teams, the American Football League sprang up in 1960 to rival the NFL. The two leagues merged in 1966, but still played their own schedules. The top teams from both leagues met in a championship game that soon became the Super Bowl.

In 1970, a conference system was set up. Teams from the original league combined to make the National Football Conference (NFC). Most of the teams from the American Football League were housed in the new American Football Conference (AFC).

Since 1972, pro football has been more popular than Major League Baseball or college football. Fans have packed stadiums and the NFL has prospered financially.

14

Pride and Joy

A better scoreboard was part of the 2012 deal that kept the Bills playing at Buffalo's Ralph Wilson Stadium.

Since NFL teams give a city **prestige**, economic benefits, and civic pride, competition for **franchises** is fierce. Fans in Baltimore and St. Louis saw their teams depart for rival areas (Indianapolis and Phoenix) and diehard fans in Cleveland were left with an **expansion team** when the franchise was shifted to return pro football to Baltimore.

NFL teams sometimes use the threat of relocation to gain improvements for their facilities. Fans so feared the possibility of the Buffalo Bills moving to Toronto that city, county, and state officials agreed to pay the team $95 million for stadium upgrades, even though the Bills were already very profitable.

Home of the Greats

There is no greater honor for an NFL player than to be chosen for membership in the hall of fame. The NFL agreed to locate the hall in Canton, Ohio because the NFL's initial meeting was held there. Only about 300 players and coaches have been chosen for membership. Players must be retired for at least five years before they can be awarded the golden jacket that comes with **induction**.

15

GOING FOR THE SUPER BOWL TROPHY

The road to the Super Bowl is never easy. First, teams must prepare for the regular season with four preseason games in late summer. Teams start with a maximum of 90 players, but the team can only put 53 on the opening-day **roster**. Then, the team must survive a tough 16-game schedule that begins in early September. Each team plays eight home games. Since winning in a **hostile** stadium is so difficult for visiting teams, a team usually must win most of their home games to have any chance of qualifying for the playoffs or postseason.

NFL players work hard to keep their skills sharp. They begin training camp in late July for each new season.

CATCH THIS!

Only one team, the 2010 Seattle Seahawks, has made it to the playoffs with a losing record. They had seven wins and nine losses.

Clash of Champions

January is playoff time in the NFL. Six teams from each conference, made up of four division winners and two wild card teams (clubs that did not win the division but still had excellent records), play off to decide the Super Bowl contestants.

The month kicks off with the Wild Card Weekend, with two games in each conference between wild card teams and conference opponents. The survivors advance into the divisional final and then the conference championship game a week later. After a week's rest for the newly crowned AFC and NFC champions, the two teams meet in the Super Bowl.

What They Play For

The original design for what would become the Vince Lombardi Trophy was drawn on a napkin by the vice president of Tiffany & Co. during a lunch with then-NFL commissioner Pete Rozelle. In 1970, four years into its life, it was renamed the Vince Lombardi Trophy after the legendary Green Bay Packers coach. Unlike hockey's Stanley Cup, a new Vince Lombardi Trophy is produced by Tiffany each season. While it is made of sterling silver, the trophy is pretty light. It weighs only seven pounds (3kg).

The Seattle Seahawks raise the Lombardi Trophy after winning the Super Bowl in 2014.

17

Green Bay Packers

The Green Bay Packers, coached by Vincent Lombardi and quarterbacked by Bart Starr, won the first two Super Bowls with scores of 35-10 in the first, and 33-14 in the second. That established "the Pack" as the first **dynasty** in the Super Bowl era.

The NFC's Packers won the first Super Bowl against the AFC's Kansas City Chiefs in 1967.

Bart Starr was named Most Valuable Player (MVP) in both the first and second Super Bowls.

Miami Dolphins

With their 14-0 regular season record, two straight playoff wins, and then a 14-7 win over Washington in the 1973 Super Bowl, the 1972 Miami Dolphins became the measuring stick for greatness. The Dolphins lost only two regular season games when storming to their second straight Super Bowl win the following season.

Pittsburgh Steelers

The 1970s belonged to the mighty Pittsburgh Steelers, who tore through the NFL winning four Super Bowls in six years. Pittsburgh's defense, nicknamed the Steel Curtain, featured four eventual hall-of-famers—"Mean" Joe Greene, Jack Ham, Jack Lambert, and Mel Blount.

San Francisco 49ers

The San Francisco 49ers rode the arm of quarterback legend Joe Montana to Super Bowl championships in 1982, 1985, 1989, and 1990. Joe Montana threw 122 passes in those four championships, and was never intercepted.

Joe Montana (16) and his head coach Bill Walsh (right) both became hall-of-famers.

Super Bowl rings are a gift from the NFL, not the individual teams.

Ring Bearers

While they cost about $5,000 each to produce, Super Bowl rings are priceless to many players because they represent the struggle to reach the peak of NFL success. The rings are usually made of gold and contain diamonds. They are one of a kind because they contain the player's name and uniform number. Charles Haley, an outstanding **pass rusher**, has five rings, giving him the record for most rings as a player.

19

Buffalo Bills

One of the most consistently excellent teams of the 1990s never won a Super Bowl. The Buffalo Bills appeared in the 1991, 1992, 1993, and 1994 Super Bowls, but lost all four.

Dallas Cowboys

The Bills were twice beaten by the Dallas Cowboys at the Super Bowl. They lost 52-17 in 1993, and 30-13 in 1994. The Cowboys won their third Super Bowl of the decade by beating Pittsburgh in 1996.

CATCH THIS!

Winning consecutive Super Bowls is seldom achieved. No team has done it since the 2005 Patriots.

Larry Brown (24) was the first cornerback to win Super Bowl MVP. He made two interceptions for Dallas in the 1996 game.

San Francisco 49ers

One of the NFL's most successful franchises, the San Francisco 49ers, said goodbye to quarterback great Joe Montana and rebuilt their team around the more youthful quarterback Steve Young. Young threw a record six touchdown passes in the 1995 Super Bowl to lead "the Niners" to their fifth championship.

After being Joe Montana's backup, Steve Young stepped up and was Super Bowl MVP in 1995.

Indianapolis Colts

In 2007, quarterback Peyton Manning led the Indianapolis Colts to a Super Bowl victory. Manning led the Colts to the playoffs for nine consecutive seasons.

Eli Manning of the New York Giants was Super Bowl MVP in 2008 and 2012, after his big brother Peyton won in 2007.

New England Patriots

The 2007 New England Patriots won all 16 of their regular-season games, but they were beaten 17-14 by the New York Giants in the Super Bowl.

Tom Brady of the New England Patriots won Super Bowl MVP in 2002, 2004, and 2015.

PRO FOOTBALL IN CANADA

Football's roots in Canada extend back to the popularity of rugby in the late 1800s. In 1869, the Hamilton Football club was formed, eventually becoming the present-day Tiger-Cats. Four years later, the Toronto Argonauts were formed.

Canadian Football League

By the 1920s, pro football teams had formed in several Canadian cities. They played each other regularly, but did not form an official league until 1958, when the Canadian Football League (CFL) began. The CFL is a nine-team league, with the BC Lions, Edmonton Eskimos, Calgary Stampeders, Winnipeg Blue Bombers, and Saskatchewan Roughriders in the Western Division. The Eastern Division is home to the Hamilton Tiger-Cats, Toronto Argonauts, Ottawa Redblacks, and Montreal Alouettes.

Since 1948, neighboring teams Toronto and Hamilton have played a huge rivalry game every September called the CFL's Labour Day Classic.

Different Rules

The basic game is the same, but the CFL and NFL have some big differences. The most important one is the number of downs. In the NFL, a team has four chances to gain 10 yards and a first down. The Canadian game features three downs in which a team can gain another first down, score a touchdown, or kick either a **field goal** or a single point. CFL fields are longer and wider than the ones used in the NFL. CFL **end zones** are 20 yards (18 m) instead of 10 yards (9 m) deep. Since there are fewer downs and more room for offenses to operate, CFL teams usually have a more passing-oriented offense than NFL teams, which usually aim for a mix of running and passing.

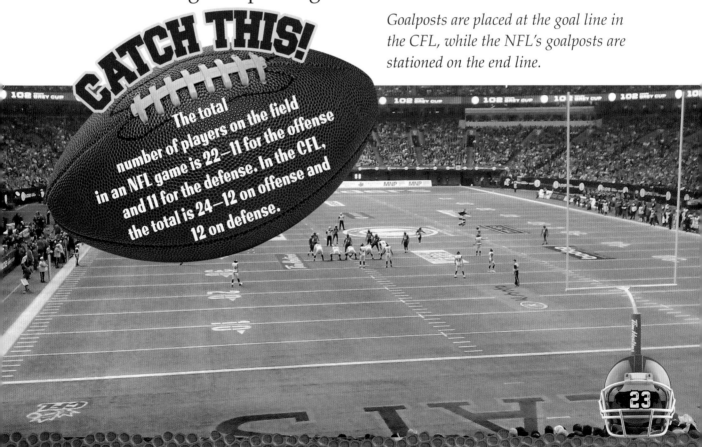

CATCH THIS!

The total number of players on the field in an NFL game is 22—11 for the offense and 11 for the defense. In the CFL, the total is 24—12 on offense and 12 on defense.

Goalposts are placed at the goal line in the CFL, while the NFL's goalposts are stationed on the end line.

23

THE GREY CUP

The winners of each division in the CFL play for the Grey Cup on the last Sunday in November. Thousands of fans flock to the host city for a week of parties. Millions more watch the championship game on TV. The CFL plays 18 regular-season games, then three weeks of playoffs. The first-place teams in each division get a week off, while the second-and third-place teams play to see who will advance. If a fourth-place team from one division has a better record than a third-place team from the opposite division, the team with the better record "crosses over" into the other division playoff.

CATCH THIS!

The Toronto Argonauts have won 16 Grey Cups, the most by any franchise in CFL history.

Flags, bands, and a special halftime show are part of the fun at the Grey Cup game.

Beloved Trophy

The trophy was created by Albert Grey (1851-1917), the Governor General of Canada. Albert Grey wanted his trophy to be awarded to the country's best hockey team, but when that honor was already taken, he donated it to amateur rugby. Canada's pro football teams have been competing for the Grey Cup since 1954. Each year, players on the winning team take the Cup to their hometowns to celebrate. The beloved trophy also toured Canada by train for its 100th anniversary as fans lined up to see it.

The Grey Cup was first won by the University of Toronto Varsity Blues in 1909.

Once in a Lifetime

Convinced that expansion into the United States was key to the league's survival, the CFL welcomed four American franchises from 1993 to 1995. The game did not catch on, but the move resulted in the only Grey Cup champion from an American city. Relying on CFL veterans, the Baltimore Stallions defeated Calgary 37-20 in the 1995 championship game. The Stallions folded when NFL football returned to Baltimore and the franchise was relocated to Montreal.

The CFL uses a replica as well as the original Grey Cup to save on wear and tear. Together, the two Cups have been broken six times, stolen twice, and damaged in a fire.

AMERICAN FOOTBALL IN EUROPE

American football has crossed over to Europe in the last 100 years or so, where the game has become very popular. Many Europeans got a good look at the game when they saw American and Canadian soldiers playing their versions of football on military bases during and after World Wars I and II.

Starting in the 1970s, football began to take off in Europe. Europe is presently home to more than 2,000 teams playing American-style football, in leagues that range from youth to adult. Britain boasts 22 first-division clubs, while Germany has 17, Italy and Sweden both have 11 teams, and Ireland and Portugal each have 10.

In Europe, it's hard to beat the Vikings. The Vienna Vikings, that is. The Vikings have won a record five European titles and finished as runners-up another five times in their 40-plus year history.

Running the Show

Europe now has its own football organization, the European Federation of American Football (EFAF). EFAF runs leagues for players of all ages, title games, and even cheerleading championships. Football associations from 30 different nations belong to EFAF. The top club teams face off in the annual Eurobowl. The EFAF Cup is another big American-style football tournament.

Unlike NFL and CFL players, European players are usually not paid.

NFL in Europe

In an effort to boost its popularity in Europe, the NFL sponsored two professional leagues, but the ventures eventually failed. The NFL has proven most popular in London, where three sold-out games were played in 2015. The NFL hopes to have a team in London by 2022. A major problem facing the league is the gap between time zones. Fans in New York would have to get up at 8:30 a.m. to catch a 1:30 pm game in England. Although, some football fans might enjoy a football Sunday that runs from breakfast to almost midnight.

Banners on busy Regent Street show how popular the NFL has become in London.

27

EUROPEAN CHAMPIONSHIPS

The top teams in the BIG6 European Football League play for the Eurobowl. In the first year of the tournament, three of the BIG6 members were based in Germany, with two more in Austria and one in France. Organizers are hoping to bring in teams from more countries to create a truly European championship. Two German teams faced off for the 2015 Eurobowl Championship. The New Yorker Lions defeated the Schwabisch Hall Unicorns to win the title in front of 5,000 fans in Braunschweig, Germany.

HYPO NOE LOUNGE

The Swarco Raiders celebrated winning the Eurobowl in 2008, 2009, and 2011. They were also the runners-up in 2013. The powerful Austrian squad shares team colors and a partnership with the Oakland Raiders. Swarco is the only European team with an NFL partner.

28

BritBowl

The top teams in the United Kingdom compete for the BritBowl. These teams play in the Premier Division of the British American Football Association Community Leagues (BAFA). Title games are also held for lower divisions of BAFA. The London Warriors won their third straight title in the 29th BritBowl in 2015. Since 2011, the Warriors and London Blitz met in the final for five straight years.

The London Blitz senior team won both the Brit Bowl and the EFAF Cup in 2011.

Austrian Bowl

The Austrian Football League (AFL) has four teams from Austria and one from the nearby Czech Republic. After a 10-game season, the top two teams meet in the Austrian Bowl. The AFL is a tough league, and AFL teams often win the Eurobowl and other big tournaments.

The Vienna Vikings (in yellow) and Swarco Raiders have a big rivalry going in the Austria Bowl. Vienna won in 2013 and 2014, but Swarco got revenge by winning in 2015.

GETTING INTO THE BIG GAME

Do you dream of holding the Vince Lombardi Trophy or the Grey Cup? Now is the time to start your journey.

In the United States, football is widely played by elementary school-aged athletes. More than one million American boys and nearly 2,000 girls compete in 11-player tackle football every year. Of those, one quarter play Pop Warner youth football, which is open to players aged five to 14.

Football is also extremely popular in high school. In Canada, 900 high school teams play the 12-player version of the sport, and there are more than 14,000 high school teams in the United States. If you practice and improve your skills, you will be ready to make that key block, tackle, or run to help your teammates. Success in football is based on dedication, hard work, and teamwork. It's time for you to get into the game!

Football teammates often become lifetime buddies.

LEARNING MORE

There are many books you can read and websites you can visit to learn more about football.

Books

What Is the Super Bowl? by Dina Anastasio, c. 2015, Penguin Random House

Fantastic Sports Facts, Football Record Breakers by Michael Hurley, c. 2013, Capstone Press

The College Football Championship by Matt Doeden, c. 2015, Millbrook Press

Websites

Pop Warner Football
www.popwarner.com/football

This site has information about joining a team and staying safe as you play.

NFL
www.nfl.com

The NFL website has information on all the NFL teams including scores, schedules, standings, and more. It also has links at the bottom of the page for other NFL sites.

GLOSSARY

clamored Made a loud or strong demand

dynasty A family or team that is very powerful or successful for many years

end zone The area just past the goal line

expansion team A new franchise, started from scratch, that begins play in the NFL

field goal A score of three points is made by kicking the football through the crossbar

forward pass An action in which the football is thrown so that it ends up further down the field than it is at the place where it is thrown from

franchise A team or business authorized by a larger organization to operate in a particular area

hoists Raises or lifts up

hostile Relating to an enemy, unfriendly or harsh

induction Official act of making someone a member of a group

Midwest A region of the north-central United States around the Great Lakes and the upper Mississippi Valley

minimize Make smaller

pass rusher A defender whose job is to pursue the quarterback across the line of scrimmage

prestige Respect and admiration in the eyes of other people

rivalries Situations where people or teams are competing with teach other

roster The official list of players on the team

roughing the passer Making illegal contact with the quarterback after the ball is released

semifinal A round of games preceding the final one in a tournament from which losing teams are eliminated

system of downs Series of usually four downs in which a team must gain 10 yards to keep the ball

INDEX